13

CÉZANNE

LANDSCAPES

PETITE ENCYCLOPÉDIE
DE L'ART

CÉZANNE

LANDSCAPES
BY
JOHN REWALD

TUDOR PUBLISHING CO.

NEW-YORK

Most of the Impressionists went abroad at some time or other. Manet travelled in Spain, Pissarro in England, Renoir in Algiers and Sicily, Monet in Holland, Italy, England, and Scandinavia; Degas went as far afield as New Orleans, and Gauguin to the Tropics. Cézanne certainly had the means and opportunity to travel, but although he greatly admired the works of the Venetian masters, he never went to Italy, or even to Belgium to see the paintings of his beloved Rubens. He knew little even of France outside his own province; he lived for some years, off and on, in and around Paris, but it was for reasons of health that he went to Vichy, and to please his wife that he spent a summer on the shores of the lake of Annecy, whence he wrote to a fellow-Provençal: "It's all right, of course, but it can't compare with our own part of the country—if you have been born *there*, it's finished—there just isn't any other place for you."

Cézanne was passionately attached to Provence, and particularly to the country around Aix, not only because he had spent his early years there—a happy, sunny time, full of great plans and greater hopes—but also because the character of the Provençal landscape was peculiarly stimulating to an artist who could express his emotions only in terms of colour and form. Yet he had no great affection for the citizens of Aix, who considered that the son of a rich banker who insisted on painting must be eccentric, if not actually mad, and despised him accordingly. "The way things are," wrote Cézanne bitterly in 1896 to his friend Joachim Gasquet, "the best thing I could do would be to slip quietly away, and if I didn't love the country so much, I shouldn't be here."

All his friends eventually settled in new homes —Pissarro at Éragny, Monet at Giverny, Renoir in the South, Zola at Médan; but Cézanne remained faithful to the region where he was born, with its infinite variety of landscapes bathed in the clear yet soft light of the Provençal sun.

He attempts to capture the beauty of Provence in some of his very earliest pictures, setting up his easel beside the River Arc or beneath the tall chestnut-trees of his father's estate, the Jas de Bouffan. Soon he was working exclusively on landscapes. In 1886, he wrote to Zola from Aix: "No picture painted indoors, in a studio, can compare with the things you can do in the open air. When you paint an outdoor scene, you get astonishing contrasts, and the landscape is magnificent. It's wonderful; I must make a resolution to work only in the open air... I have a strong suspicion that all the pictures of the old masters showing outdoor scenes are artificial; they don't seem to me to have the true and, above all, the perpetually new appearance of nature itself."

In another letter, also written in 1866, this time to Pissarro, his friend and fellow-artist, he says: "You are right in what you say about grey; it is the dominant colour in natural landscape, but it is terribly hard to capture it. The country is very beautiful here, very impressive." So Cézanne, in his own home on the outskirts of Aix, and at the age of twenty-seven, had already experienced that "contact with nature" which he was later to proclaim indispensable to the development of art, at the very time when, in the North, Monet and his friends were laying the foundations of Impressionism.

Cézanne had only to look over the wall of the Jas de Bouffan, which appears in the foreground of *The Cutting* (Pl. 2) to be confronted with a

LANDSCAPE. PENCIL DRAWING. 1880-1885.

dazzling view, and the richness of the colouring of this picture shows how strongly it affected him. He has not yet learnt to restrain his enthusiasm, to tone down the blue of the sky or the sombre tints of the shadows on the ground; he emphasises the marvellous beauty of this Midi landscape by deliberate exaggeration. As for the grey which is "the dominant colour of natural landscape," he has not yet succeeded in capturing it, though he has already realised that he can do so only by using a number of different colours.

After the war of 1870, Cézanne worked for some time with Pissarro in Pontoise and Auvers, where he developed a clearer and more subtle style, and when he returned to Provence, he saw it with different eyes. Whereas his early works express his first enthusiastic reaction, the later pictures are the products of a patient study of nature. In his Parisian landscapes, he had at last discovered the secret of the troublesome grey, made up of a multitude of different shades, and by a technique of tiny, juxtaposed strokes he now tries to reproduce it in all its inexhaustible variety. He had learnt that there is no such thing as a "local colour"; the effect of the air between the eye and the object, and the light reflected from other objects must be taken into account. This stage in his development is best illustrated by *The House of the Hanged Man* (Pl. 3), painted at Auvers-sur-Oise.

The fruit of Cézanne's Parisian experiences, both visual and technical, appears in the pictures he painted on his return to the Jas de Bouffan; they constitute a virtual rediscovery of Provence.

LANDSCAPE WITH A BRIDGE. DRAWING.
1895-1900.

He sees it now in terms of coloured planes organised in a firm, almost architectural construction, irreconcilable with the doctrines of Impressionism.

Wherever Cézanne went in the serenely beautiful countryside around Aix, he could be sure of finding grandiose vistas, brilliant colours, and picturesque forms. From a hilltop, for example, he could look over an immense valley to the conical summit of Mount Sainte-Victoire. In such a landscape, the dominant forms are so massive that the details are reduced to insignificance, and the large planes and clearly-traced line—such as those of a viaduct with open arches—lent themselves admirably to the fulfilment of Cézanne's purpose, which was "to paint like Poussin, but from nature." These unobstructed yet enclosed panoramas were not to be found in the North, but in Provence he had a rich and harmonious landscape always ready to hand. It was in "subjects" of this kind that he set out to solve the problems of space and colour which preoccupied him at this time, and was thus able to remain faithful to nature while searching for new means of conveying his impressions. "I am trying to express perspective entirely through colour," he explained at the end of his life.

He often worked in Gardanne, a small town not far from Aix, situated on a hillside and dominated by a church with a tall steeple (Pl. 6); and only a little further away, at L'Estaque, was the sea. In his youth, Cézanne had spent many happy holidays by the Mediterranean, and he never tired of the magnificent bay of Marseilles, surrounded by mountains, the tiny villages with their bell-towers and tall chimneys pointing towards the cloudless sky, the pine-clad hills, and the rocky islets standing out against the azure sea and stretching away to the horizon (Pl. 4 and 5). In a letter to Pissarro, Cézanne says of this wonderful panorama: "It's like a playing-card. Red roofs against a blue sea. The sun is so strong that every object seems to be silhouetted not only in black and white, but in blue, red, brown, purple... I may be wrong, but it seems to me to be the exact opposite of modelling."

But L'Estaque was fast becoming an industrial town, and Cézanne rarely returned there after 1885. He spent much of his time in the Jas de Bouffan and in the neighbourhood of Aix, painting isolated houses hidden behind trees

LANDSCAPE. PENCIL DRAWING. 1880-1885.

(Pl. 8), steeply-rising roads, twisted pines (Pl. 15), and cottages with cracked walls (Pl. 10). He was forced to sell the family estate in 1899, after which he often worked in the Bibémus quarry, and at Château-Noir, with its wilderness of rocks and trees spread over the broad hillside. *The Winding Road* (Pl. 13) shows the approach to Château-Noir, with the grey, majestic wall of Mount Sainte-Victoire in the background.

It was not until 1901, five years before his death, that Cézanne decided to build a studio just outside Aix. He continued to live in town, but was usually in the studio at five o'clock in the morning, working in the garden on portraits, still-lifes, and above all his big pictures of women bathing, whose settings always represent, in a more or less idealised form, the banks of the little River Arc where he had spent so many carefree hours in his youth. But in the afternoon he would climb the Colline des Lauves behind his studio to a point from which he could overlook the wooded valleys at the foot of Sainte-Victoire. Seen from this angle, the mountain slopes gently on one side, sharply on the other. Here, with broad strokes of the brush, and larges splashes of thick, heavy paint, Cézanne would recreate the landscape in a multitude of infinitely varying and interacting shades of colour. This bold, authoritative style was the culminating triumph of a long life of constant experiment, from which later generations were to profit, sometimes in quite unexpected ways.

To this day, the countryside around Aix still bears the impress of Cézanne's personality. It

THE ROOFS OF L'ESTAQUE. PENCIL DRAWING.
c. 1880.

is *his* landscapes we come upon round every bend, on every path, in front of every pine or rock; for the artist was so completely one with his native region that we can no longer see it through any eyes but his.

LIST OF PLATES

3

5

6

8

ACHEVÉ D'IMPRIMER
EN FÉVRIER 1958 PAR J.-M. MONNIER
CLICHÉS PERROT ET GRISET